The Colonel Stephens

Peter A. Harding

Hawthorn Leslie 2-4-0T No.2 "Northiam" at Tenterden Town Station on the Kent & East Sussex Railway, with a mixed train for Headcorn. July 22nd 1938. R.F.Roberts

Published by Peter A. Harding
Mossgiel, Bagshot Road, Knaphill
Woking, Surrey GU21 2SG

ISBN 0 9509414 9 2

© Peter A. Harding 1993
*Printed by Binfield Printers Ltd.,
Binfield Road, Byfleet, Surrey KT14 7PN*

Contents

	Page No.
Introduction	3
Holman Fred Stephens	4
The Cranbrook & Paddock Wood Railway (Later the Hawkhurst Branch Line)	12
The Rother Valley Railway (Later the Kent & East Sussex Railway)	16
The Sheppey Light Railway	22
The East Kent Light Railway	25
Conclusion	31
Acknowledgments/Bibliography	32

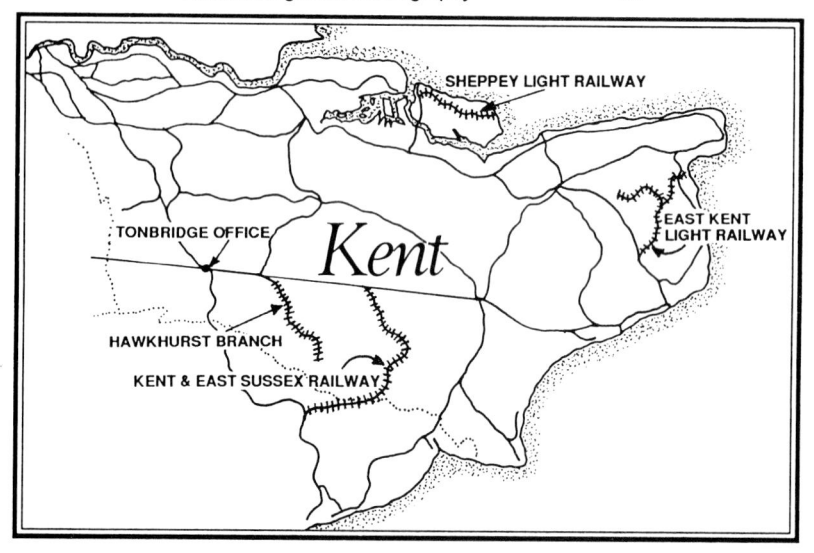

C class 0-6-0 No.31592 pulls a goods train through the orchards on the Hawkhurst branch line between Horsmonden and Paddock Wood on May 19th 1961. The line was originally opened in 1892 by the Cranbrook & Paddock Wood Railway. J.J.Smith

Introduction

In 1890, the young and enterprising Holman Fred Stephens set out on his long career by taking on the responsibility as resident engineer to the Cranbrook & Paddock Wood Railway in Kent, where he gained much valuable experience. Although he later went on to plan, build and manage many minor railways in all parts of the country, it was while working on the Cranbrook & Paddock Wood Railway that he appears to have developed an affinity with the county of Kent. It was at Cranbrook (and later Tonbridge) that he set up his home and headquarters, and where he was involved with the construction of four railways in the county, and had plans for many others which were never built.

With the passing of the Light Railway Act in 1896, Stephens soon became a major figure, who's engineering skills and management were always in demand. Having gained the rank of Lt. Colonel in the 1914-18 war, the lines which he managed were often referred to as "The Colonel Stephens Railways", and although he is remembered as the head of this rather quaint group of light railways, which he controlled on a shoe-string budget from his office at Tonbridge, he also had many revolutionary ideas which are sometimes overlooked by enthusiasts and historians alike.

The charm and fascination of the railways managed by Holman Fred Stephens belong to a bygone age, when the very pace of life was far more leisurely. I hope that this booklet will be a suitable reminder of those tranquil days of the Colonel Stephens Railways in Kent.

The wayside station at Wingham,Canterbury Road on the East Kent Light Railway, epitomizing the very spirit of the Col. Stephens railway empire. September 23rd 1947.   R.F.Roberts

Holman Fred Stephens
(1868-1931)

Col. Stephens Railway Museum, Tenterden

Born in Hammersmith, London on October 31st 1868, Holman Fred Stephens was the son of the art critic Frederic George Stephens who was a founder member of the pre-Raphaelite Brotherhood and his wife Rebecca Clara. Affectionately known to his family as "Holly", the young Stephens was named after the artist William Holman Hunt, who was a friend of his father and also a fellow member of the pre-Raphaelite Brotherhood.

From 1877 until 1883, young Holly attended University College School in London and, following a spell with a private tutor, his parents decided to send him to the continent to further his education. First, in 1884, he went to France, where he studied French at Vitré in Brittany until 1886, and then in 1887 to Karlsruhe (Baden) in Germany, where he studied German and Mathematics. On returning to England later in 1887, he took his matriculation at London University.

After taking his matriculation, Stephens studied civil engineering under Sir Alexander Kennedy at University College, London until 1888, and finished his education from 1889 until 1890 with some practical experience at the Metropolitan Railway workshops and locomotive department at Neasden Works, where he studied mechanical engineering under Mr.J.J.Hanbury who was at that time resident engineer and locomotive superintendent to the Metropolitan Railway.

During the whole period of his education and with the choice of his future career, the young Stephens received every encouragement from his parents and it seems that there was no pressure for him to follow his father into the world of art and literature where Frederic George Stephens (1828 - 1907) had been an influential figure during the mid to latter part of the nineteenth century. Although F.G.Stephens was never considered a great artist, he did exhibit portraits at the Royal Academy in 1852 and 1854, before gaining a reputation as art critic to *The Athenaeum* from 1861 to 1907, after he had championed the claims of Dante Gabriel Rossetti to the initiation of the pre-Raphaelite Brotherhood. Other activities involving F.G.Stephens included, contributing to *The Germ* (the art magazine of the pre-Raphaelite movement) and he was also the model for the head of Christ in the famous painting "Christ Washing Peter's Feet" by Ford Madox Brown.

From the railway workshops at Neasden, the young Holman F. Stephens embarked on his long career as an engineer, general organiser and in many cases managing director of various minor railways throughout the country. At the age of 22, he took up his first appointment in 1890, at Cranbrook in Kent, where he set up his home and base as resident engineer to the Cranbrook & Paddock Wood Railway. One of the reasons he became involved with this particular railway was probably due to the fact that the consulting engineer was Edward P. Seaton who, like Stephens, was also connected to the Metropolitan Railway at Neasden, where he acted as an independent consultant, later becoming the Metropolitan's resident engineer from 1903 to 1905 when he retired through ill health.

Even while he was involved with the Cranbrook & Paddock Wood Railway, Stephens still kept in touch with the Metropolitan Railway by assisting with alterations at Baker Street and also the construction of the Kings Cross Subway. He also found time in 1894 to become a Board of Trade Inspector (under notice of Accident Act), a position he held on a part time basis for several years.

Although the Cranbrook & Paddock Wood Railway was built by an independent company, it was supported and worked by the South Eastern Railway who soon stepped in and purchased the line after it was completed from Paddock Wood to Hawkhurst, and from then on, Stephens had no further dealings with the day-to-day running of the railway, although he had made several important aquaintances which were to hold him in good stead in the years to follow.

In 1895, after a short commission with the Cranbrook & District Water Company, Stephens moved on to his next railway appointment which was engineer to the 3ft gauge Rye & Camber Tramway in Sussex. The contractors for this short line were Mancktelow Bros. of Horsmonden, who laid the track and built the station buildings. Mancktelow Bros. had in fact been responsible for the station buildings on the Cranbrook & Paddock Wood Railway, although they did not lay the track.

As Cranbrook was rather remote for other planned lines in Kent and beyond, Stephens decided to look for a more central base, and in November 1895 he established an office and home at Ashby House, Priory Road, Tonbridge, where he employed William Henry Austen as his assistant. Austen was originally engaged while he was in his early teens, by Stephens at Cranbrook in 1891, during construction of the Cranbrook & Paddock Wood Railway. He also went on to help Stephens with the Rye & Camber Tramway.

The ceremonial first train at Hope Mill Station (which was later re-named Goudhurst) on Monday September 12th 1892. Holman Fred Stephens is the tall man with light trousers, standing next to the locomotive.
Col. Stephens Railway Museum, Tenterden

Holman Fred Stephens (left) with the local Squire and Vicar at Hope Mill Station on the same day.
National Railway Museum

Having completed the Rye & Camber Tramway, the association between Stephens and Mancktelow Bros. continued in 1897 when they were appointed engineer and contractor respectively to the Hundred of Manhood & Selsey Tramway, also in Sussex.

An interesting deviation to Stephens' railway work at about this time was the maintenance and renewal of 13 locks on the Upper Navigation of the River Medway, all very close to his Tonbridge office and home.

The passing of the Light Railway Act of 1896 was ideal for the type of railway which Stephens was now involved with and he was soon in demand with various light railway schemes and proposals from all over the country. He even engineered one of the first light railways to be constructed under the provisions of the 1896 Act, which was the Rother Valley Railway, running from Robertsbridge in Sussex to Tenterden in Kent. Later, this line was extended from Tenterden to Headcorn and renamed the Kent & East Sussex Railway. Apart from being the lines engineer, he soon became the managing director.

Holman Fred Stephens (fourth from left) with his team of surveyors at Tenterden, during the planning stages of the Rother Valley/Kent & East Sussex Railway.

Col. Stephens Railway Museum, Tenterden

By early 1900, Stephens was heavily involved with lines which he had either completed and was managing, or were at the drawing board stage, and he decided that the time was right to move his office in Tonbridge from Ashby House in Priory Road, which had become too small for his growing "empire", to No. 23 Salford Terrace, not too far from Tonbridge Station. In fact, his telegraphic address was quite simply "Stephens, Tonbridge Station". Although he moved his office, Ashby House remained his home until his death, even though he spent much of his time at rented rooms in Station Road, Robertsbridge, and often stayed at various hotels, including the Queens Hotel in Hastings, the White Lion in Tenterden, and also for a long period at the Lord Warden Hotel in Dover.

While involved with his first project, the Cranbrook & Paddock Wood Railway, it appears that Stephens became acquainted with Edward I.W. Peterson, a solicitor working in the Cranbrook area, and between them they helped form the Light Railway Syndicate which promoted light railways throughout the country.

The office at 23 Salford Terrace, Tonbridge in 1937.   Author's Collection

Although the early part of the century was a very successful period for Stephens, the Light Railway Syndicate was unfortunately not, even though it was successful in promoting the Sheppey Light Railway on the Isle of Sheppey. By 1912, the Syndicate were voluntarily liquidated after several schemes in Essex failed to materialise, mainly because Peterson was unable to raise the necessary finance.

The Sheppey Light Railway was the third line in Kent to be built by Stephens and was opened in 1901, but, like the Cranbrook & Paddock Wood Railway, this line was also never to form part of his group and was worked from the outset by the South Eastern & Chatham Railway, who absorbed the line in 1905, making the Sheppey Light Railway the only light railway in their whole network.

The fourth and final Kentish line which Stephens constructed was the East Kent Light Railway, which was mainly built to serve the Kent coalfields. Coal was first discovered when the borings for the original Channel Tunnel scheme were made in the latter part of the nineteenth century.

Although the East Kent Light Railway was the last railway which Stephens actually built in Kent (even though it was never fully completed), he certainly had plans for many others. The one line which looked as though it would be built was an extension of the Kent & East Sussex Railway from Headcorn to Maidstone but, through one reason or another, it never was, even though Stephens had obtained a special locomotive (Hawthorn Leslie 0-8-0T named 'Hecate') possibly to work this section.

A party of specially invited guests at Leysdown Station on August 9th 1901, to commemorate the opening of the Sheppey Light Railway which had officially opened on August 1st 1901.
Author's Collection

The ceremonial first train on the East Kent Light Railway, which ran from Shepherdswell to Tilmanstone Colliery on November 27th 1912. Seen here at Tilmanstone Colliery, the locomotive is Fox Walker 0-6-0ST No.1. Holman Fred Stephens is in front of the telegraph pole.
Col. Stephens Railway Museum, Tenterden

Other lines planned by Stephens in Kent (or partly) which never materialised were as follows:- The Hadlow Light Railway; the Cranbrook, Tenterden & Ashford Light Railway; the Orpington, Cudham & Tatsfield Light Railway; the Maidstone & Faversham Junction Light Railway; the Maidstone & Sittingbourne Junction Light Railway; the Sandwich Tramway; and the Southern Heights Light Railway.

Although these lines came to nothing, the staff at 23 Salford Terrace, Tonbridge, certainly had their hands full controlling the lines which Stephens had built and was managing from all over the country, plus other lines which he had either reconstructed or acquired to form his group. The full list read as follows:- The Kent & East Sussex Railway; the East Kent Light Railway; the Hundred of Manhood & Selsey Tramway (later called the West Sussex Railway); the Shropshire & Montgomeryshire Light Railway; the Weston, Clevedon & Portishead Railway; the Festiniog Railway; the Welsh Highland Railway; and the Snailbeach District Railway. He also built and managed the Plymouth, Devonport & South Western Junction Railway, but later resigned from the management position due to other commitments.

At any one time, 12 people were employed at 23 Salford Terrace, with two or three allocated to each line. Everyone had to work hard with unpaid overtime expected at any time. Wages were less than the main line companies and it was strickly forbidden for any member of the staff to join a trade union. Stephens seems to have been well liked by his employees but, he could be very impatient at times. He had a railway type internal telephone system in the office, with bell codes for each person. If he failed to get an answer straight away, he would get very irritated and quickly call again.

Other lines which he engineered, but never formed any part of his Tonbridge managed group were as follows:- The Burry Port & Gwendraeth Valley Railway, the Ashover Light Railway, the Edge Hill Light Railway, the North Devon & Cornwall Junction Railway, the Weston Point Light Railway, and of course the previously mentioned Cranbrook & Paddock Wood Railway, the Sheppey Light Railway and the Rye & Camber Tramway.

In 1911, Stephens was even appointed engineer to the Isle of Wight Central Railway but, after a few months he found that his weekly visits to the island to carry out his duties were taking up too much of his valuable time, and he resigned.

During the 1914-18 war, Stephens acquired the rank of Lieutenant Colonel after he had raised and commanded 2,400 men and 220 officers, while serving with the Royal Engineers (TR), and he was also mentioned in despatches in 1916.

When he returned to full time railway work in 1916, he celebrated by taking his whole Tonbridge office staff to the Criterion Restaurant on February 4th, followed by a visit to the Lyceum Threatre, and from this time onwards, he was always known as 'Colonel Stephens'.

A tall man of commanding presence, he could be very kind and would often hand out tips or cigars on a visit to one of his railways if he felt that his staff had done well, but if he thought the opposite, a short sharp memo would soon follow, telling the particular person to "pull up their socks or else". The late George Dobell worked on the Kent & East Sussex Railway from 1917 until it closed to passengers in 1954, and said that they always knew when the "Colonel" was about. A wink from the engine driver was enough to say that he was on the train. If he had his bowler hat over his eyes, you kept out of his way, because he was in a bad mood. If his hat was square on his head, he was in a good mood.

As might be expected, there was a certain amount of locomotive and rolling stock exchange between the Stephens managed group of railways, and in some cases even the staff moved from one of his railways to another.

While planning motive power for the Rye & Camber Tramway, Stephens had explored the possibility of working the line with an 'oil motor on a passenger bogie car' and, although the idea did not appeal to the management, who favoured a conventional steam locomotive, the idea was never lost. In the 1920's, when road competition was an ever increasing threat to his group of light railways, Stephens became interested in using petrol driven railbuses. After experimenting with a Wolseley-Siddeley motorcar, fitted with a bus-type body and flanged wheels, on the Kent & East Sussex Railway, he must have been encouraged with the results because he ordered three pairs of railbuses for that line. These railbuses resembled pairs of small road buses, coupled back-to-back so that they could be driven from either end without the necessity of a turntable at the end of a journey. The first two sets were Model T Fords and were supplied by Edmonds of Thetford, while the other one was built by Shefflex Motors of Sheffield. Similar railbuses were used on all Stephens' standard gauge lines except, surprisingly, the East Kent Light Railway.

In 1923, Stephens was offered the chance of grouping his lines into the 'Big Four' companies but, characteristicly he declined, preferring to hang on to his mini 'empire' and remain independent.

At about this time, he became a permanent resident of the Lord Warden Hotel in Dover and, despite the fact that in the late 1920's he had suffered a stroke which paralysed the right side of his body and deprived him of his speech, he still travelled most days by train to his Tonbridge office and even visited some of his "far flung" railways.

He died at the Lord Warden Hotel on Friday October 23rd 1931, when he was 63 years old, and was buried in the family grave at Brompton Cemetary, Fulham Road, London.

As there were no surviving relatives, four members of the Salford Terrace staff shared equally in Stephens estate of some £30,000. They were W.H.Austen, J.A.Iggulden, A.Willard and G.H.Willard. The family collection of mainly pre-Raphaelite paintings were bequeathed to the Tate gallery.

At the time, there was some speculation as to what would happen to the Stephens group of light railways, but, W.H.Austen soon took control and although the days of the light railway was very much in decline, he managed to keep going until nationalisation in 1948, when the doors of No.23 Salford Terrace finally put up the shutters to this rather quaint, but very endearing assortment of minor railways.

The Shefflex railbus set at Rolvenden on the Kent & East Sussex Railway. May 5th 1935.
J.H.L.Adams/J.Scott-Morgan Collection

The Cranbrook & Paddock Wood Railway (Later the Hawkhurst Branch Line)

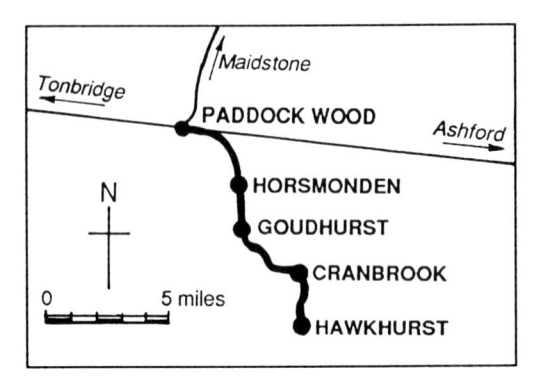

Although rich in hop growing, the high ridges and deep valleys of the Weald of Kent were not ideally suitable for the development of railways, but, nevertheless, the area did receive several schemes, ranging from Headcorn to Rye in 1844, Paddock Wood to Rye Harbour in 1854, Headcorn to Tenterden via Cranbrook in 1855, and Marden to Cranbrook via Goudhurst in 1857.

The first serious proposal was in 1864 by the Weald of Kent Railway, for a line from Paddock Wood to Hythe via Cranbrook and Tenterden. Although powers were obtained, the project failed to get off the ground until 1877, when a new company, called the Cranbrook & Paddock Wood Railway, was incorporated to build the northern section of the previously proposed Weald of Kent Railway. The line was to run from Paddock Wood (on the main line between Tonbridge and Ashford) to Cranbrook via Horsmonden and Goudhurst.

In 1882, the company obtained a second act to extend the line from Cranbrook to Hawkhurst, although this extension was modified in 1892 to divert it along a less severely graded route. The terminus was now to be over a mile north of Hawkhurst, at a place called Gills Green, 11½ miles from Paddock Wood.

The line opened on Monday September 12th 1892 from Paddock Wood via Horsmonden to Goudhurst (then known as Hope Mill Station for Goudhurst and Lamberhurst) and was finally opened through to Hawkhurst via Cranbrook on Monday September 4th 1893.

The Cranbrook & Paddock Wood Railway was worked from the outset by the South Eastern Railway, who, by 1900, had absorbed the company into their system, and the line gradually became known as the Hawkhurst branch line. The South Eastern Railway had, by that time, ended their bitter rivalry with the London, Chatham & Dover Railway by negotiating an arrangement whereby both companies remained separate, but worked together under the heading of the South Eastern & Chatham Railway Management Committee.

This was the first line that Holman F. Stephens was actually involved with as an engineer and, although it was built as a conventional branch line and operated from its opening by the South Eastern Railway, it still had one or two traits which were to appear in some of the light railways which he later built and managed. The contractor who was responsible for track laying and earthworks, was J.T.Firbank, while the stations, which included a rather grand stationmasters house, two of which (at

Goudhurst and Cranbrook) were actually built on the station adjoining the station building, were constructed by Mancktelow Bros. of Horsmonden.

Passenger services were originally worked by Cudworth E class 2-4-0's, followed by Stirling Q class 0-4-4T's, and occasionally Stirling F & B class 4-4-0's. After the First World War, the South Eastern & Chatham Railway introduced the Kirtley R class 0-4-4T's, and by the 1930's, the R1 class 0-4-4T's. The R & R1's worked the passenger service until the mid 1950's, when they were withdrawn and replaced by the Wainwright H class 0-4-4T's, which were mainly used on the line until it closed.

Goods trains were pulled in earlier times by Stirling O class 0-6-0's, but soon after the First World War, Wainwright C class 0-6-0's were introduced and continued to work the line until its closure, although in latter days the Paddock Wood diesel shunter was sometimes used.

After the 1923 grouping, the South Eastern & Chatham Railway became part of the newly formed Southern Railway and, although things did not change much, by 1948, when the line passed into the hands of the newly formed British Railways Southern Region after nationalisation, it became obvious that the branch was living on borrowed time. Although used and remembered with much affection by hop pickers, farmers, a few local people and railway enthusiasts alike, the railway never really made much money, and by the early 1960's, when the hop picking traffic ceased, it was not much of a surprise when the announcement came that the line would close.

The Hawkhurst branch officially closed on Saturday June 10th 1961, although the following day a special train, organised by the Locomotive Club of Great Britain, and called "South Eastern Limited", went down the branch to Hawkhurst and back, then later the same day, the remaining portion of the Kent & East Sussex Railway from Robertsbridge to Tenterden. This train was the last public service train to run to and from Hawkhurst.

Horsmonden Station, soon after the line had opened.   Lens of Sutton

H class 0-4-4T No.31543 approaching Horsmonden Tunnel. May 19th 1961. J.J.Smith

C class 0-6-0 No.31271 at Cranbrook Station. September 22nd 1951. R.F.Roberts

R class 0-4-4T No.31675 at Hawkhurst Station. September 22nd 1951. R.F.Roberts

The impressive stationmaster's house at Goudhurst Station, which was built on the platform, adjoining the station building. May 22nd 1961. J.J.Smith

E4 class 0-6-2T No.32580 with a 'hop-picker' special train at Cranbrook Station. September 22nd 1951. R.F.Roberts

Hawkhurst Station, looking towards the buffer stops. August 3rd 1946. R.F.Roberts

The Rother Valley Railway
(Later the Kent & East Sussex Railway)

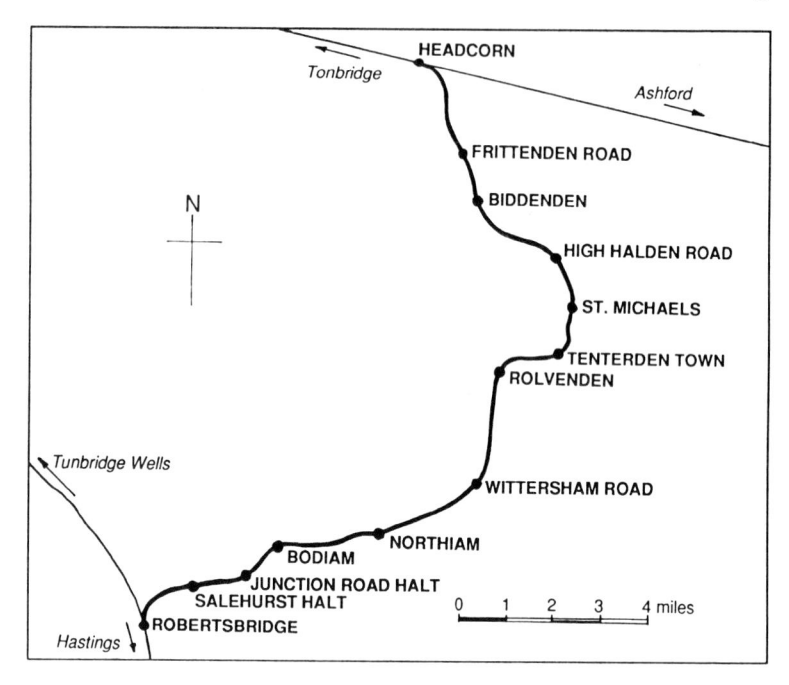

In many ways, the Tenterden area received the same attention as the early proposals involving the Cranbrook & Paddock Wood Railway but, it was not until 1896 that the Rother Valley Railway took advantage of the recently passed Light Railway Act to build a line, 12 miles long, from Robertsbridge in Sussex (on the main Tonbridge to Hastings line) to a terminus between Rolvenden and Tenterden in Kent, which was to be called Tenterden Station.

With his previous experience in the area, it was not so surprising that Holman F. Stephens was appointed engineer, and he soon set about designing this new line, which would cross the rather remote Rother Valley. The contract for building the line was given to the London & Scottish Contract Corporation, who in turn sub-contracted the work to Godfrey & Siddelow.

The Rother Valley Railway opened from Robertsbridge to Tenterden, for goods traffic on March 26th 1900, and for passengers on April 2nd 1900. The line was extended by 1½ miles on March 16th 1903, from the original Tenterden Station, which was then renamed Rolvenden, to a new station near the town centre of Tenterden, which was appropriately named Tenterden Town. On May 15th 1905. the line was extended by a further 8 miles, from Tenterden Town to Headcorn (on the main Tonbridge to Ashford line) and was renamed the Kent & East Sussex Railway. The full length of the line was 21½ miles. The contractor, for the short extension from the original Tenterden Station to Tenterden Town and the longer extension to Headcorn, was William Rigby.

Although there were several plans for further extensions from the Kent & East Sussex Railway, ranging from Robertsbridge to Pevensey, Northiam to Rye, Headcorn to Maidstone, plus a plan to link with the Hawkhurst branch at Cranbrook, nothing further was built and the Kent & East Sussex Railway was now complete.

Holman F. Stephens went on to become managing director of the company and many people believe that it was his favourite railway. Certainly, it was the nearest of his independent railways to the Tonbridge office.

In 1923, Stephens declined the offer of grouping his lines into the new 'Big Four' companies and the Kent & East Sussex Railway was left to survive in its own sweet way but, after Stephens' death in 1931, W.H.Austen took control, and somehow managed to kept the line going until nationalisation in 1948, when it became part of the newly formed British Railways Southern Region.

The new owners took a more realistic view of the line, and even improved the track and signalling etc., but when traffic receipts did not come up to expectations, they quickly decided to withdraw the passenger service entirely, and leave only a goods service between Robertsbridge and Tenterden. The section of line between Headcorn and Tenterden would be taken out of use altogether. The final passenger service ran on Saturday January 2nd 1954, although the goods service remained until the line was officially closed on June 11th 1961, when the special train, organised by the Locomotive Club of Great Britain and called "South Eastern Limited", went up from Robertsbridge to Tenterden and back, after it had carried out a similar duty on the Hawkhurst branch.

Two Hawthorn Leslie 2-4-0T's were obtained for the line when it was first opened and, duly became No.1 "Tenterden" and No.2 "Northiam". In May 1901, a Stroudley Terrier 0-6-0T No.70 "Poplar", was obtained from the London, Brighton & South Coast Railway, and became No.3 "Bodiam". In 1904, Hawthorn Leslie supplied an 0-8-0T, for possibe use on the proposed Headcorn to Maidstone section and this locomotive became No.4 "Hecate", but it was too heavy for the existing route and, as the Maidstone section was never built, it was rarely used. Later it was loaned to the East Kent Light Railway, before it was sold in 1932 to the Southern Railway, with ex-London & South Western Railway Beyer Peacock 0-6-0ST No.335, coming as part exchange. Another Terrier, No.671 "Wapping", was bought from the London, Brighton & South Coast Railway in 1905, and became No.5 "Rolvenden".

Terrier 0-6-0T No.3 "Bodiam" at Headcorn Junction, with a train for Tenterden. July 8th 1938.

R.F.Roberts

No.6 on the locomotive list was a steam railcar, supplied by R.Y.Pickering of Lanarkshire in 1905, but it was not a success and was allowed to decay at Rolvenden. In 1910, an 0-6-0 tender locomotive of the London & South Western Railway Ilfracombe Goods class, was obtained, and became No.7 "Rother". No.8 was a Manning Wardle 0-6-0ST, obtained from the Bute Works Supply Company in 1914, and was named "Hesperus".

Another Ilfracombe Goods was purchased in 1914 from the London & South Western Railway, and this locomotive became No.9 "Juno".

Before nationalisation in 1948, the Kent & East Sussex Railway hired a number of locomotives from the Southern Railway. These would either be Wainwright P class 0-6-0T's, Stroudley Terrier class 0-6-0T's, Stirling O1 class 0-6-0's, Adams 0395 class 0-6-0's, or 0330 class 0-6-0ST's.

In British Railways days, the Headcorn-Tenterden section was worked by, first the 0395 class 0-6-0's, and then, mainly the O1 class 0-6-0's. The Tenterden-Robertsbridge section was handled by the Terriers, which also occasionally worked the Headcorn section as well.

When the Headcorn section was closed, the Terriers handled all goods services until the arrival of the O4 class diesels, and even then the Terriers returned to help and also work any 'Specials'.

As mentioned previously, Colonel Stephens was very interested in petrol driven railbuses, and the Kent & East Sussex Railway obtained three sets for use on their line. Two of these sets were Model T Fords and were obtained from Edmonds of Thetford, one in 1923 and the other one in 1924, while the third set was paid for by Stephens himself in 1929 and came from Shefflex Motors of Sheffield.

Shefflex railbus set at Rolvenden shed in May 1939.   The late S.W.Baker

The line also had an interesting collection of carriages, some new from Hurst Nelson when the line opened, while many were secondhand from main line companies. The most fascinating was a former London & South Western Railway 'Royal' carriage, which had been displayed at the Great Exhibition of 1851. In 1908, this carriage, with an earlier royal carriage of 1844, had been obtained by the Plymouth, Devonport & South Western Junction Railway while Stephens was engineer to that line. Later he obtained the 1844 carriage for the Shropshire & Montgomeryshire Light Railway, while the 1851 carriage went to the Kent & East Sussex Railway, where it was sometimes used by Stephens as an inspection vehicle, although, as it was for a time the only carriage with lights, it was often used for night working.

The former London & South Western Railway 'Royal' carriage at Rolvenden in 1930.
The late H.C.Casserley

Ilfracombe Goods class 0-6-0 No.9 "Juno", seen leaving Rolvenden with a single carriage train for Robertsbridge on August 19th 1933.
The late H.C.Casserley

Hawthorn Leslie 2-4-0T No.2 "Northiam", with a single carriage train, waits for passengers at Headcorn, the junction station for the Kent & East Sussex Railway. July 22nd 1938.   R.F.Roberts

The wooden platform at St.Michaels. April 11th 1953.   S.C.Nash

O1 class 0-6-0 No.31064 with a single carriage train at Tenterden Town Station in the early 1950's.   John H.Meredith

Terrier 0-6-0T No.3 "Bodiam" pulling away from Tenterden Town towards Headcorn. June 19th 1948.
John H.Meredith

Southern Railway P class 0-6-0T No.1556 at Rolvenden Station while on loan to the Kent & East Sussex Railway. March 26th 1938.
R.F.Roberts

The Sheppey Light Railway

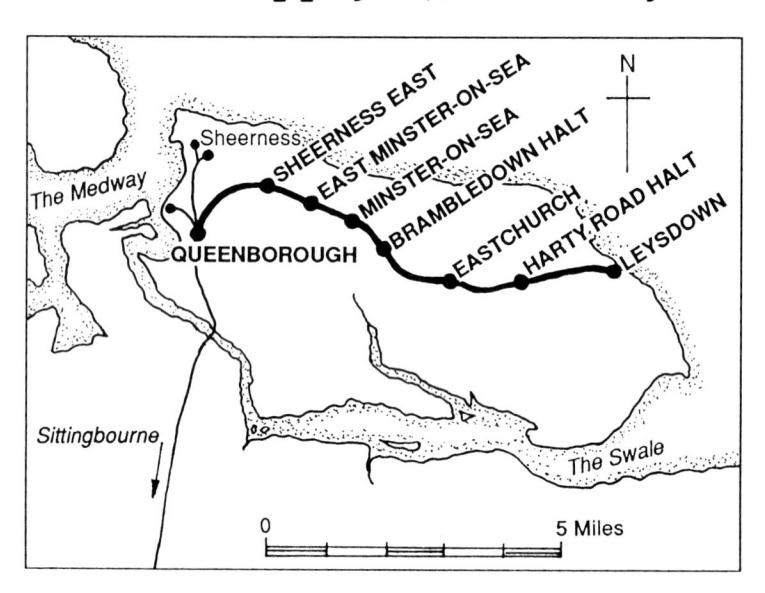

When the idea for a light railway on the Isle of Sheppey was first proposed, Holman F. Stephens was involved from the very early stages, by way of Lord Medway, who was one of his acquaintances from the Cranbrook & Paddock Wood Railway. In 1896, Lord Medway had given Stephens a letter of introduction to Lord Harris of Belmont Park, Faversham, who was an influential landowner on the Isle of Sheppey and, with encouragement from other interested parties on the island, the Light Railway Syndicate (which Stephens had formed a year earlier with the Cranbrook based solicitor Edward I.W. Peterson) was asked to plan and organise a line which would benefit all concerned.

The original proposal from Stephens was for a line to run south from Queenborough Station, on the Sittingbourne to Sheerness line, in an easterly direction across the southern marshes to Leysdown. Before an enquiry was held, it was clear that this route did not meet with local approval and, after various wishes were taken into consideration, it was decided to divert the route. The new route went to the north of Queenborough Station, trailing out to the east and coming within a mile of the east side of Sheerness, at an area known as Halfway House, and within a 1/2 mile of Minster at Scocles Road, then rejoining the original planned route, which was just south of Eastchurch and on to Leysdown, 8 3/4 miles from Queenborough.

An enquiry was held before the Light Railway Commissioners at Queenborough on April 29th 1898 and the order was confirmed on April 3rd 1899. The contractor appointed to build the line was William Rigby, and the line officially opened on August 1st 1901.

From opening, the line was worked by the South Eastern & Chatham Railway, who used Neilson built Scotchmen class 0-4-2WT's and R&W Hawthorn built Sondes class 2-4-0T's. By 1905, the South Eastern & Chatham Railway had absorbed the line and decided to carry out trials with railcars. First, two small petrol-electric railcars, built by Dick, Kerr & Co, were tried, but proved to be unsuitable but then the Wainwright designed steam railcars were used with more success. In 1905, the South Eastern & Chatham Railway decided to order from the London, Brighton & South Coast Railway, a Stroudley Terrier class 0-6-0 No.751 called "Waddon", for goods duties. This engine soon became a great favourite with the islanders, who nicknamed it "Little Tich" after the well known music hall star of the day.

Later, Stirling O class 0-6-0's took over the goods duties and, during the 1914-18 war, even the passenger service.

In the early 1920's, a Stirling Q class 0-4-4 took over the passenger service, followed by the Sharp Stewart built Kirtley R & R1 class 0-4-4T's, which were to work the line until closure, with the occasional help of Stirling B1 class 4-4-0's, Wainwright E class 4-4-0's, and the ever faithful Wainwright C class 0-6-0's.

Originally, carriages used on the line were London, Chatham & Dover Railway six-wheel saloons, fitted with vestibules and low footboards, and these vehicles remained in service until 1924. From then on the carriage portions of the former Wainwright steam railcars, No's.1, 2, 3 and 8, were paired as two articulated sets for use on the line until it closed.

In 1923, the line passed into the hands of the Southern Railway at the time of grouping, and in 1948, became part of the British Railways Southern Region after nationalisation. The new owners soon decided that the railway was not paying its way and, despite opposition from local people, including the Sheerness Urban District Council, the line closed completely, on and from Monday December 4th 1950.

R1 class 0-4-4T No.31705 in the Sheppey Light Railway bay at Queenborough Station on December 2nd 1950, the last day of public service. Dr. E.Course

Eastchurch Station, looking east towards Leysdown.   Lens of Sutton

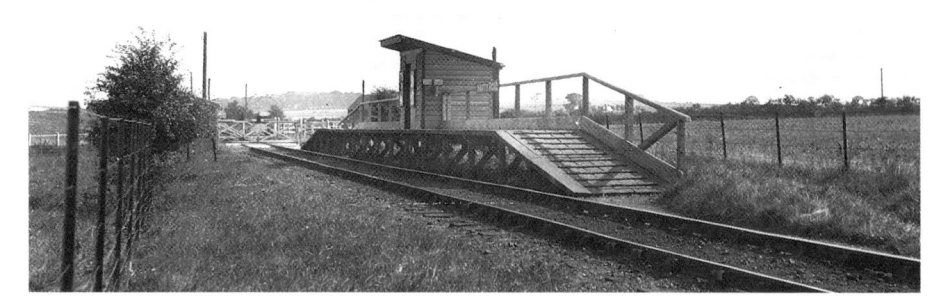

Harty Road Halt.   Lens of Sutton

R1 class 0-4-4T No.31698 backing onto articulated set No.513 at Leysdown Station. March 4th 1950.   D.Trevor Rowe

The East Kent Light Railway

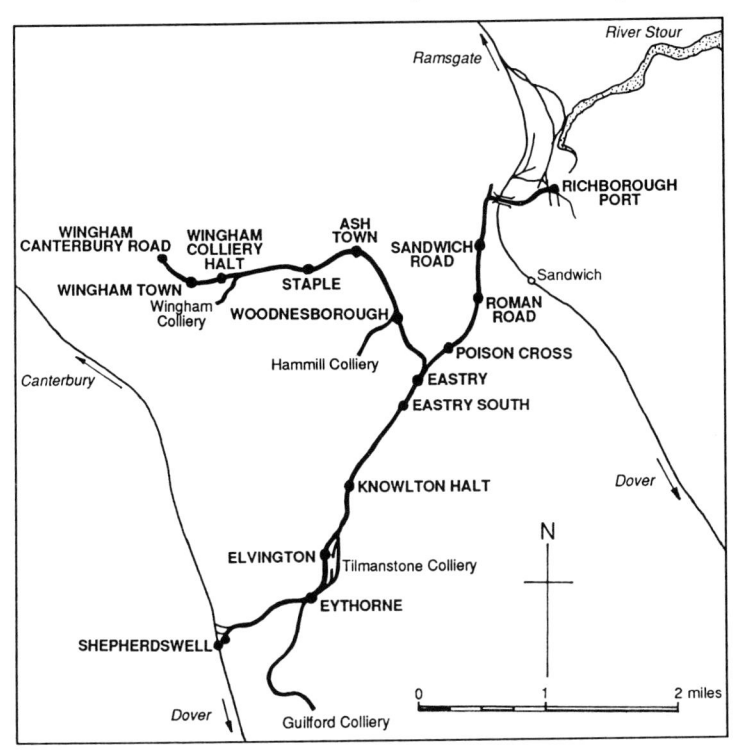

The East Kent Light Railway was originally promoted in 1910, by a group of colliery owners known as the Kent Coal Concessions, in conjunction with other independent colliery owners to serve the newly discovered Kent coalfields, which came to light when trial borings were carried out for the Channel Tunnel in 1882, at Shakespeare Cliff, near Dover.

Once coal was discovered, the Channel Tunnel took a backward step and over 40 borings were sunk in and around the area. Collieries were quickly established at Tilmanstone, Guilford, Stonehall, Snowdown, Goodmanstone, Chislet and Wingham, with many others soon to follow.

The original plans were for the new railway to run from the main Canterbury to Dover line at Shepherdswell via Eastry, to the west bank of the River Stour at Richborough, where hopefully a wharf would be built so that coal could be exported. A branch would run from this new line at Eythorne, to Guilford Colliery, plus a branch to Tilmanstone Colliery, which would rejoin the new proposed railway to form a loop. At Eastry, the line would fork with the original line, going on to Richborough, and another line would turn north to connect with the main Canterbury and Ramsgate line between Canterbury West and Sturry via Wingham, making the whole system over 30 miles of track.

A public enquiry was held at Canterbury in October 1910, and 11½ miles of the original application was withdrawn. This mainly included the section between the main Canterbury and Ramsgate line, and Wingham. A revised application was made to the Board of Trade in February 1911, and a Light Railway Order was confirmed on June 19th 1911.

With his vast experience with similar lines, Holman F. Stephens was a natural choice as engineer, and the contract for the construction work was placed with the East Kent Contract and Financial Co. Ltd. By December 1911, a temporary line had been laid from Shepherdswell to Tilmanstone Colliery, which went around Golgotha Hill (the main obstacle in the area), while a tunnel was bored through the hill, and a long cutting dug. When the tunnel and cutting were completed, the temporary line was removed. Although Golgotha Tunnel was built for double tracks, only one track was laid, while the space for the second track was not fully excavated, leaving blocks of solid chalk standing for most of the length of the tunnel.

By October 1912, the line had reached Eastry, which was to be the junction for the Richborough and Wingham sections, while the short branch to Guilford Colliery, from Eythorne, was also completed by this date. The line from Eastry to Wingham Colliery (with a short branch to Hammill Colliery) was constructed later the same year, although the 1/2 mile extension to Wingham Town was not built until 1920.

Unfortunately, by 1914 some of the smaller collieries, including Wingham and Hammill, had closed. When war was declared in August 1914, the company sought permission to open the line to passenger traffic, and this request was granted. Minimal facilities were provided, with basic platforms, and the line opened to passengers in October 1916, from Shepherdswell to Wingham. Also, in the same year, the War Department decided to develop Richborough as a major seaport but, although they were quite well advanced, the East Kent Light Railway had unfortunately not reached Richborough at this time. The main obstacle was the building of a bridge to cross over the road to Richborough Castle, the River Stour and the main Dover and Ramsgate railway line. In the meantime, the Richborough line was opened to passengers in August 1925 from Eastry, but only as far as Sandwich Road, south of Richborough Castle, with intermediate stations at Poison Cross and Roman Road. After the bridge was completed in 1928, a station was built at Richborough Port, but never received any passengers, as the bridge was not approved for passenger traffic.

Looking towards the buffer stops at Shepherdswell Station, showing goods wagons. September 24th 1938.
R.F.Roberts

As it was, by that time Richborough had ceased to be a major seaport and the War Department had sold it to Pearson, Dorman Long, who were not over enthusiastic on dealing with the East Kent Light Railway and delayed the opening of the goods service until 1929. By then, the passenger service between Eastry and Sandwich Road had already been withdrawn, on October 31st 1928.

There were many plans to extend the East Kent Light Railway during the course of its existence, mainly in the earlier years, to link with the numerous other collieries, which in the end were never actually built. The company still had plans to extend their line from Wingham Town to Canterbury, and also to link with Deal, plus a scheme to build a line to a new port proposal at Birchington, but unfortunately the only extension, apart from the long awaited Richborough Port line was in 1925, when the Wingham line was extended just over 1½ miles to a new station, originally called Wingham and later Wingham, Canterbury Road. A short cutting was made in the direction of Canterbury, but no further work was carried out ,and from then on, the East Kent Light Railway was as complete as it ever would be.

When the railways were nationalised in 1948, the line became part of British Railways Southern Region, and to reduce losses, the entire passenger services were withdrawn on November 1st 1948. The Richborough line closed completely on October 27th 1949, the Wingham,Canterbury Road to Eastry section closed on July 25th 1950, and the line north of Eythorne closed on March 1st 1951. Coal traffic from Tilmanstone continued until April 1984, although the line officially closed on December 31st 1987.

Like all Colonel Stephens managed railways, the East Kent Light Railway had an interesting miscellaneous collection of locomotives, ranging from the Fox Walker 0-6-0ST, which was obtained from the Bute Docks Supply Co., and was used by the contractors during construction later becoming locomotive No.1, and the Hudswell Clarke built 0-6-0ST, which came from another Col. Stephens line – the Weston, Clevedon & Portishead Railway, and became No. 2. In fact, as with other Col. Stephens railways, the East Kent Light Railway received several locomotives,either

Level crossing near Shepherdswell, looking towards Eythorne. September 23rd 1947. R.F.Roberts

on loan or permanently, from other lines in his group. Another interesting locomotive was the former London & South Western Railway, Adams designed Radial tank 4-4-2T, which was obtained from the Ridham Salvage Depot at Sittingbourne, and became No.5.

During the latter days of the line, the motive power was normally a Stirling O1 0-6-0, while the final workings up to Tilmanstone Colliery were made by Class 73 Electro-Diesels.

At the opening in 1912, a bogie vestibule carriage was obtained from R.Y.Pickering, and when the line later opened to passengers, four 4-wheel and six 6-wheel carriages were obtained secondhand from main line companies.

O1 class 0-6-0 No.6 at the East Kent Light Railway station at Shepherdswell, ready to leave for Wingham, Canterbury Road. September 23rd 1947.
R.F.Roberts

Hudswell Clarke 0-6-0ST No.2 "Walton Park" at Shepherdswell Station with a mixed train for Wingham, Canterbury Road on June 30th 1934.
The late H.C.Casserley

Eastry South Station, looking towards Eastry. Lens of Sutton

Eastry Station. The line to Richborough carries on straight ahead, while the line to Wingham, Canterbury Road turns off to the left. Lens of Sutton

Wingham, Canterbury Road Station. Author's Collection

Roman Road Station, looking towards Richborough. March 4th 1951. S.C.Nash

Sandwich Road Station, looking towards Richborough. March 4th 1951. S.C.Nash

Richborough Port Station, which never received any passengers. Lens of Sutton

Conclusion

The four lines which Holman Fred Stephens was involved with in Kent, all kept their original charm and character right up until closure, maintaining a service to rural parts of the county which had never previously been accessible. Unfortunately, with the improvement of road transport, they were never able to compete with road buses which could take passengers to the centre of a village or town, while many stations on light railways and branch lines would often be a mile or two from the place they claimed to service. Nevertheless, the railway was always held in much affection by local people, farmers and railway enthusiasts alike, and even today, over thirty years after the last of the four lines in Kent officially closed for passengers, they are still remembered with the same fondness.

Fortunately, a large part of the Rother Valley section of the Kent & East Sussex Railway is in the hands of the Tenterden Railway Company, a preservation company who have set about the task of restoring the line to at least some of its former glory and presently run a service between Tenterden and Northiam, with the eventual aim of not only reaching Bodiam, but also, possibly the main line at Robertsbridge. Another interesting feature is the Col. Stephens Museum, which the company have set up as part of the Tenterden Museum in Station Road, where the Colonel's original desk and relics can be seen.

Also, the more recently formed East Kent Light Railway Society hopes to preserve and operate the section between Sheperdswell and the site of Tilmanstone Colliery.

A timeless scene on the preserved Kent & East Sussex Railway as Terrier 0-6-0T No.10 "Sutton" approaches Tenterden Town Station on June 2nd 1991. Author

Acknowledgments

I would like to thank John Scott-Morgan for all his help and encouragement and for making his photographic collection so readily available to me. Thanks also to Philip Shaw for allowing me to make use of the "Tenterden Terrier" (of which he is the editor) and to John Miller for the use of photographs from the Col. Stephens Railway Museum.

I would also like to thank the following people and organisations for their kind help in supplying photographs:- Mr.R.F.Roberts, Mr.S.C.Nash, Mr.J.J.Smith, Mr.R.M.Casserley, Mr.J.H.Meredith, Dr.E.Course, Mr.D.Trevor Rowe, Mr.D.T.Agate, Mr.J.L.Smith (of Lens of Sutton) and the National Railway Museum.

Thanks once again to my son Paul for reading my text and to Mr.J.O.Christian of Binfield Printers for his help.

Bibliography

THE COLONEL STEPHENS RAILWAYS by John Scott-Morgan *(David & Charles)*
RAILWAYS OF ARCADIA by John Scott-Morgan *(P.E.Waters & Associates)*
THE KENT & EAST SUSSEX RAILWAY by Stephen Garrett *(Oakwood Press)*
THE EAST KENT RAILWAY by A.R.Catt *(Oakwood Press)*
RAILS TO TENTERDEN by J.L.Smith *(Lens of Sutton)*
BRANCH LINE TO TENTERDEN by Vic Mitchell & Keith Smith *(Middleton Press)*
BRANCH LINE TO HAWKHURST by Vic Mitchell & Keith Smith *(Middleton Press)*
THE EAST KENT LIGHT RAILWAY by Vic Mitchell & Keith Smith *(Middleton Press)*
RAILWAY MAGAZINE (Various issues)
THE TENTERDEN TERRIER (Various issues)

The former Kent & East Sussex Railway station at High Halden Road on April 7th 1993.
D.T.Agate